World War II
and the Post-War Years

By
MARIA BACKUS

COPYRIGHT © 2002 Mark Twain Media, Inc.

ISBN 1-58037-217-1

Printing No. CD-1563

Mark Twain Media, Inc., Publishers
Distributed by Carson-Dellosa Publishing Company, Inc.

The purchase of this book entitles the buyer to reproduce the student pages for classroom use only. Other permissions may be obtained by writing Mark Twain Media, Inc., Publishers.

All rights reserved. Printed in the United States of America.

Table of Contents

1. About the American History Series
2. Time Line of World War II and Post-War Events
3. The Rise of Dictators
4. The German Dictator
5. The Italian Dictator
6. The Japanese Dictator
7. Which Dictator?
8. The War Begins
9. The Persecution of the Jews in Germany
10. Britain Stands Up to Hitler
11. Should the United States Join the Allies?
12. The Attack on Pearl Harbor
13. President Roosevelt's Fireside Chats
14. America's Response
15. V is for Victory
16. Victory Gardens
17. Wartime Style
18. World War II Posters
19. Rosie the Riveter
20. What Women Did During the War
21. Women in Uniform
22. What Children Did During the War
23. The War Changes the Way Americans Live
24. Before and During the War
25. Boot Camp
26. Military Service
27. African-Americans in World War II
28. The Internment of Japanese-Americans
29. Wartime Math
30. Crossing the Atlantic Ocean
31. The Allies' Strategy
32. Planning for D-Day
33. D-Day: The Invasion of Normandy
34. The Infantry in Europe: Part I
35. The Infantry in Europe: Part II
36. The Infantry in Europe: Part III
37. A Letter Home
38. Research Projects: Part I
39. The Warplanes
40. From Ghettoes to Concentration Camps
41. Did Anyone Help the Jews?
42. Anne Frank
43. Joseph Stalin and the Soviet Union
44. V-E Day
45. Crossing the Pacific Ocean
46. The Navajo Code Talkers
47. The Japanese Invasion of the Philippines
48. Combat in Europe and in the Pacific Region
49. Iwo Jima and Ground Zero
50. President Truman's Decision
51. The Aftermath of War
52. Life in America After the War
53. The United Nations
54. The Marshall Plan
55. The Korean War
56. Research Projects: Part II
57. Famous Quotations
58. Books About World War II
59. Suggested Reading
60. Answer Keys

About the American History Series

Welcome to *World War II and the Post-War Years,* one of the books in the Mark Twain Media, Inc., American History series for students in grades four to seven.

The activity books in this series are designed as stand-alone material for classrooms and home-schoolers or as supplemental material to enhance your history curriculum. Students can be encouraged to use the books as independent study units to improve their understanding of historical events and people.

Each book provides challenging activities that enable students to explore history, geography, and social studies topics. The activities provide research opportunities and promote critical reading, thinking, and writing skills. As students learn about the people and events that influenced history, they will draw conclusions; write opinions; compare and contrast historical events, people, and places; analyze cause and effect; and improve mapping skills. Students will also have the opportunity to apply what they learn to their own lives through reflection and creative writing.

Students can further increase their knowledge and understanding of historical events by using reference sources at the library and on the Internet. Students may need assistance to learn how to use search engines and discover appropriate websites.

Titles of books for additional reading appropriate to the subject matter at this grade level are included in each book.

Although many of the questions are open-ended, answer keys are included at the back of the book for questions with specific answers.

Share a journey through history with your students as you explore the books in the Mark Twain Media, Inc., American History series:

Discovering and Exploring the Americas
Life in the Colonies
The American Revolution
The Lewis and Clark Expedition
The Westward Movement
The California Gold Rush
The Oregon and Santa Fe Trails
Slavery in the United States
The American Civil War
Abraham Lincoln and His Times
The Reconstruction Era
Industrialization in America
The Roaring Twenties and Great Depression
World War II and the Post-War Years
America in the 1960s and 1970s
America in the 1980s and 1990s

Time Line of World War II and Post-War Events

1918 World War I ends. Germany surrenders.
1921 Adolf Hitler becomes the leader of the National Socialist Party (Nazis) in Germany.
1922 Benito Mussolini becomes the dictator of Italy.
1931 Japan invades Manchuria.
1932 Franklin Roosevelt becomes President of the United States.
1934 Adolf Hitler gains absolute power as the Führer of Germany.
1937 Japan invades China.
Japan, Germany, and Italy sign Axis Powers treaty.
1938 Germany annexes Austria.
1939 Germany annexes Czechoslovakia and then invades Poland in September. World War II begins.
Great Britain, France, Australia, New Zealand, and Canada declare war on Germany.
Germany and the Soviet Union sign a non-aggression pact. They divide Poland between them.
1940 Winston Churchill becomes Prime Minister of Britain.
Denmark, Norway, the Netherlands, Belgium, and France fall to Germany.
The Battle of Britain begins.
1941 Germany breaks its agreement and invades the Soviet Union.
Japan attacks Pearl Harbor on Dec. 7.
The United States and Britain declare war on Japan.
1942 The United States surrenders the Philippines to the Japanese.
Japanese-Americans on the west coast are relocated to internment camps.
The mass murder of millions of Jews begins at Auschwitz.
1943 The Allies win in North Africa.
Italy surrenders in September.
1944 The Allies invade Normandy, France, on June 6. This day is called D-Day.
Paris is liberated in August, and the Allies win the Battle of the Bulge in December.
1945 The Allies liberate Buchenwald and Bergen-Belsen concentration camps.
The United States regains control of the Philippines.
President Roosevelt dies. Harry Truman becomes president.
Mussolini is captured and hanged by Italian partisans.
Hitler commits suicide.
Germany surrenders on May 7.
May 8 is called V-E Day (Victory in Europe).
The United States drops an atomic bomb on Hiroshima, Japan, on Aug. 6 and on Nagasaki, Japan, on Aug. 9.
The United States declares Aug. 14 as V-J Day (Victory over Japan).
The United Nations (UN) charter takes effect Oct. 24.
1946 The UN General Assembly holds its first session.
Former Prime Minister Churchill gives his "Iron Curtain" speech in Fulton, Missouri.
1947 General George Marshall is appointed the U.S. Secretary of State and proposes the European Recovery Program (also known as the Marshall Plan).
World War II peace treaties are signed in Paris.
1948 The U.S. Congress approves $17 billion in aid for Europe through the Marshall Plan.
The Jewish state of Israel is created.
The Soviet Union blocks traffic between Berlin and the West. The Berlin Airlift begins.
1949 China falls to the communists.
1950 North Korean forces invade South Korea June 25 and capture Seoul.
UN forces led by General Douglas MacArthur recapture Seoul.
1951 Fighting continues in Korea, as first one side and then the other crosses the 38th parallel. Armistice negotiations begin but fail.
1952 Dwight D. Eisenhower is elected President of the United States.
1953 The Korean armistice is signed July 27. The United States and South Korea sign a mutual defense treaty.

The Rise of the Dictators

Read the information below and answer the questions.

Germany had started World War I in 1914 and lost it in 1918. The winning countries were determined to avoid future conflicts, so they placed harsh punishments on Germany. They put limits on the German military. They made Germany pay large cash payments to the winning countries, and they made Germany admit that the war was its fault. The German government became bankrupt, and the people felt humiliated.

A former German soldier named Adolf Hitler promised to make Germany a strong nation again. He declared that there would be jobs and food for everyone. He told the people that they were superior to other Europeans, and that other countries shouldn't tell them what to do. Many Germans liked what he had to say because he placed blame for Germany's troubles on others. By 1933, he was in complete control of Germany and soon became a ruthless dictator. Other countries were ruled by dictators as well. Italy was ruled by Benito Mussolini, and Japan was ruled by General Hideki Tojo.

1. What is a dictator? Check in the dictionary. Then write a definition using your *own* words.

   _____

   _____

   _____

2. What kind of personality traits do you think a dictator would have? Explain your ideas.

   _____

   _____

   _____

   _____

3. Why do you think some people might want to have a dictator rule them?

   _____

   _____

   _____

Discuss with your class: How is a dictator different from a president?

World War II and the Post-War Years

The German Dictator

Name: _____ Date: _____

The German Dictator

Adolf Hitler become the dictator of Germany in 1933. He blamed the Jews for Germany's loss in World War I even though they made up less than one percent of the population.

The majority of people in Europe were Christians. Hitler knew that he could not remove religion, so he twisted it to conform to his purposes. By using propaganda, Hitler convinced his people to blame the Jews as **scapegoats** when anything went wrong. This word means someone who is unfairly made to take all the blame for something.

Hitler's political party, the National Socialist German Worker's Party, blamed the Jews for Germany's problems.

Hitler wanted to rule all of Europe. In 1938, he invaded Austria and Czechoslovakia. He then invaded Poland in 1939. Next, Germany conquered Denmark, Norway, Luxembourg, the Netherlands, and Belgium. Hitler then defeated the French Army and marched into Paris. German planes soon began to bomb Britain.

Adolf Hitler

Use an atlas or reference book to label Germany, Austria, Czechoslovakia, Poland, Denmark, the Netherlands, Belgium, Great Britain, and France.

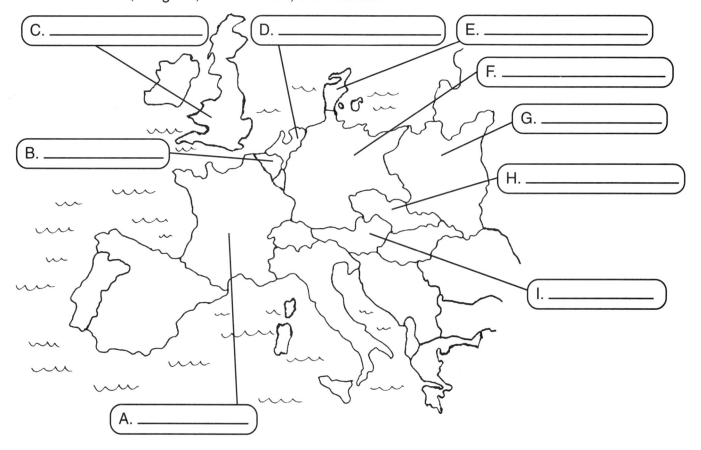

© Mark Twain Media, Inc., Publishers

World War II and the Post-War Years The Italian Dictator

Name: _____ Date: _____

The Italian Dictator

Use the words in the box to fill in the blanks. Use reference sources or the Internet to help determine the correct answers.

empire	Albania	Ethiopia	Japan
1922	Hitler	National Fascist Party	

1. When did Benito Mussolini become the dictator of Italy? _____

2. What political party did he start? _____

3. Mussolini wanted to create a great Italian _____.

4. What nation in Africa did Mussolini first invade? _____

5. What other nation across the Adriatic Sea did Mussolini invade? _____

6. In 1936, Mussolini joined forces with _____.

7. Germany and Italy became known as the Axis Powers. What other country also became part of the Axis Powers? _____

Benito Mussolini

Use an atlas or reference book to label Italy, Albania, and the Mediterranean Sea.

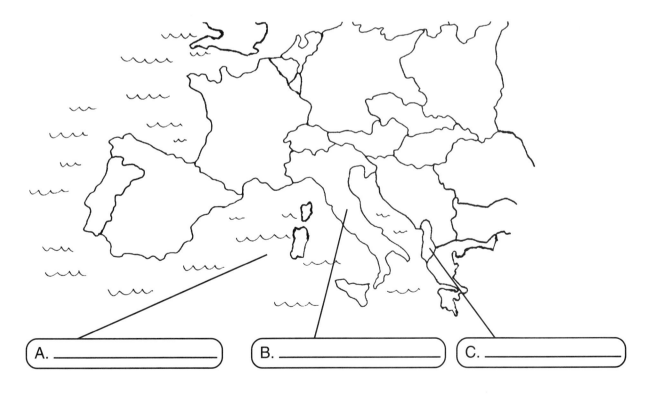

A. _____ B. _____ C. _____

© Mark Twain Media, Inc., Publishers 5

World War II and the Post-War Years

The Japanese Dictator

Name: _____ Date: _____

The Japanese Dictator

General Hideki Tojo was the Prime Minister of Japan and its Minister of War. He issued orders in Emperor Hirohito's name.

Tojo and the other military advisors wanted more land for Japan's growing population. They also wanted resources like rubber and oil that could be found in Southeast Asia.

In 1931, Japan invaded Manchuria. In 1937, Japan began a full-scale invasion of China. Ten million Chinese people died. Japan invaded Indochina in 1940.

In the fall of 1941, the United States negotiated with Japan to pull its troops out of China and other southeastern Asian countries. They refused. So the United States and Britain stopped selling oil and other goods to Japan. Japan resented this interference; in retaliation, Japan bombed Pearl Harbor, a United States naval base in Hawaii on December 7, 1941. America was suddenly drawn into World War II.

General Hideki Tojo

Use an atlas or reference book to label Japan, Manchuria, China, the Pacific Ocean, the Hawaiian Islands, and the Philippine Islands.

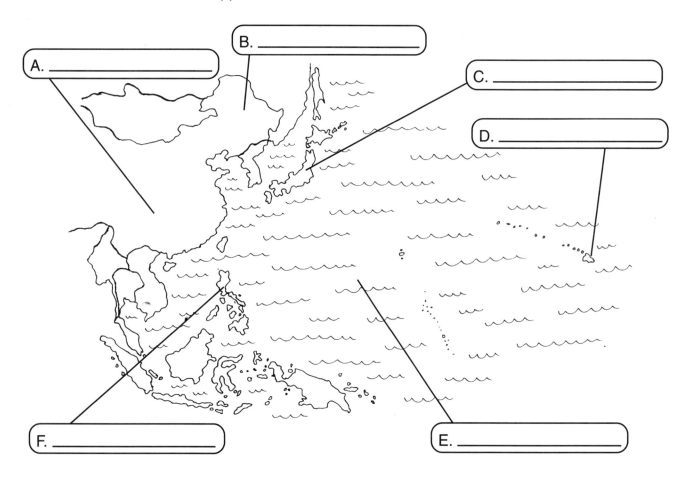

© Mark Twain Media, Inc., Publishers   6

World War II and the Post-War Years

Which Dictator?

Name: _____ Date: _____

Which Dictator?

Use what you have learned on the previous pages about Adolf Hitler, Benito Mussolini, and Hideki Tojo. Then read each statement below and decide if Hitler, Mussolini, or Tojo could have said it. In front of each statement, write an "M" for Mussolini, a "T" for Tojo, or an "H" for Hitler.

_____ 1. Germans are superior to all other Europeans.

_____ 2. I issue orders in Emperor Hirohito's name.

_____ 3. I will create a great Italian empire.

_____ 4. I invaded Albania, a country across the Adriatic Sea from Italy, in 1939.

_____ 5. I am the leader of the National Socialist German Worker's Party.

_____ 6. My country bombed Pearl Harbor and brought America into World War II.

_____ 7. To create my Italian empire, I first attacked Ethiopia in 1935.

_____ 8. The Jews are to blame for Germany's problems.

_____ 9. I want more land for Japan's growing population.

_____ 10. I started the National Fascist Party.

_____ 11. I began a full-scale invasion of China in 1937.

_____ 12. Hitler and I will rule Europe.

_____ 13. I started World War II when I invaded Poland in 1939.

_____ 14. I want the oil and rubber that can be found in Southeast Asia.

_____ 15. I invaded Austria and Czechoslovakia before I took over Poland.

GERMANY

ITALY

JAPAN

The War Begins

Read the information and fill in the blanks below.

The dictators of Germany, Italy, and Japan signed a pact in 1940 to work together to control the world. These nations were called the Axis Powers. Germany and Italy wanted to control Europe. Japan planned to take over Greater East Asia.

Germany first took over Austria and Czechoslovakia in 1938. World War II began in 1939 when Germany invaded Poland. The Allies, which at first consisted of France and Great Britain, fought against Germany. After Pearl Harbor was attacked in December 1941, the United States joined the Allies. The Soviet Union had signed a nonaggression pact with Germany, but later, the Soviet Union fought with the Allies against the Axis Powers. Eventually, two dozen nations became part of the Allies.

1. The three Axis nations: _____

2. The part of the world Germany and Italy wanted to control: _____

3. The part of the world Japan wanted to control: _____

4. The two nations that fought the Axis Powers in 1939: _____

5. The year World War II began: _____

6. The number of nations that eventually became part of the Allies: _____

7. The nation that joined the Allies in 1941: _____

8. At first, the Soviet Union signed a nonaggression pact with Germany. Later, the Soviet Union fought with the _____.

Name: _____ Date: _____

The Persecution of the Jews in Germany

Read each paragraph below. Use a dictionary to help you answer each question.

1. Adolf Hitler believed that White northern Europeans were superior and that everyone else was inferior. He believed that people in Eastern Europe were meant to be slaves. He blamed the Jews for all of Germany's troubles even though the Jews made up less than one percent of Germany's population. He even called Americans a mongrel people. What does the word *mongrel* mean?

   _____

2. Blaming the Jews was the central idea behind Hitler's National Socialist German Worker's Party (Nazis). Many Germans went along with Hitler's ideas because they were without money and jobs after World War I. They wanted to blame someone else for their troubles. The Jewish people became the scapegoats for all of Germany's problems. What does the word *scapegoat* mean?

   _____

3. Hitler soon began to persecute the Jews. In 1933, books by Jewish authors such as Albert Einstein were set on fire. Jews were banned from theaters, libraries, beaches, and entire towns. They were not allowed to vote or to work at many jobs. By 1938, Jewish children were not permitted to go to public schools. By 1941, Jews were required to wear the yellow, six-pointed Star of David on their clothes, which the Germans considered a "mark of shame." Anti-Semitic propaganda was broadcast on the radio. What does the word *anti-Semitic* mean?

   _____

4. On November 9, 1938, a Polish Jew killed a German diplomat. The Germans used this as an excuse to start a riot. That night, the *Schutzstaffel (SS)* killed 91 Jews and injured thousands more. They burned over a thousand synagogues. What is a *synagogue*?

   _____

5. The *SS* also destroyed 7,500 Jewish stores. November 9 was called Crystal Night because of all the broken glass. After that, the Nazis began to send large numbers of Jews to concentration camps. Each camp had a war business and used the Jews as slave labor. Due to the inhumane conditions, the bad food, and the lack of medicine, most workers only lasted about six weeks before they died. Jews were no longer allowed to emigrate from Germany. What does *emigrate* mean?

   _____

Britain Stands up to Hitler

Read the information and answer the questions below.

After Hitler gained control of Germany, he took over Austria and Czechoslovakia. Hitler next set his sights on Poland. The leaders in Britain and France had promised to help Poland if Hitler attacked that nation. When Germany invaded Poland in September 1939 with one million troops, Britain and France declared war on Germany. Canada also declared war on Germany.

By the end of 1940, Hitler controlled most of Europe, including Norway, Belgium, Denmark, the Netherlands, and France. Britain was the only country left to stand up to Hitler. In 1940, the Germans launched an air attack on London and other cities. This attack was called the *Blitz,* which was short for *Blitzkrieg,* a German word for "lightning war." Hitler expected Britain to surrender, but under the guidance of its new prime minister, Winston Churchill, Britain withstood the attacks.

The bombs came down on London night and day. Some parents evacuated their children from London to the British countryside where it was safer. When the air raid siren went off, people who were out in the street dashed into the subway, or "the tube." Sometimes they spent the entire night in the subway, huddled together for safety and comfort. If people were at home, they had to sit in the dark waiting for the bombing to stop.

1. What could have happened if Britain had surrendered to Hitler?

   _____

   _____

   _____

2. If you had been in Winston Churchill's "shoes," what would you have told the British people to help them continue their struggle against Hitler?

   _____

   _____

   _____

3. Why would the people at home have to sit in the dark waiting for the bombing to stop?

   _____

   _____

Name: _____ Date: _____

Should the United States Join the Allies?

As Britain fought valiantly against Germany, the United States struggled with the question of whether or not to join the Allies.

Work with a classmate. List two reasons why the United States should join the Allies and two reasons why the United States should not join the Allies.

Two reasons why the United States should join the Allies:

1. _____

2. _____

Two reasons why the United States should not join the Allies:

1. _____

2. _____

Discuss your ideas with your classmates and teacher.

Although the United States did not join the Allies at that time, it did supply them with tanks, planes, and other supplies. The United States was also concerned about Japan's invasion of China and Indochina, so it decided to halt trade with Japan. Franklin Roosevelt sent the American Pacific Fleet to Pearl Harbor so it could be closer to Japan.

Imagine that you are living in 1940. On your own paper, write an editorial that you would send to the local newspapers explaining why you think the United States should or should not join the Allies. Your paragraph should have at least five sentences including the topic sentence.

World War II and the Post-War Years   The Attack on Pearl Harbor

Name: _____ Date: _____

The Attack on Pearl Harbor

Each situation described below affected what happened next. Write the *effect* on the line. Use the Internet or other reference sources to complete the exercise.

1. On December 7, 1941, the Japanese attacked the naval base at Pearl Harbor on the Hawaiian Island of Oahu. What *effect* did the attack have on America's decision whether or not to join the Allies?

   _____
   _____

2. The attack happened at 7:55 A.M. on a Sunday morning. Many men were still asleep or eating breakfast. What *effect* did the time of the attack have on the men's ability to defend the naval base?

   _____
   _____

3. The American ships and planes were in a peacetime condition of readiness, not geared for attack. The guns were without ammunition and were unmanned. What *effect* did this have on Japan's success?

   _____
   _____

4. The American planes were an easy target because they were all parked together on the ground. What *effect* did this have on the Americans' ability to get airborne and fight back against the Japanese planes?

   _____
   _____

5. The attack destroyed America's air and sea power in the Pacific. What *effect* did that have on the Japanese ability to take control of more islands in the Pacific?

   _____
   _____

6. America declared war on Japan on December 8, 1941. Italy and Germany were Japan's allies. What *effect* did this have on America?

   _____
   _____

© Mark Twain Media, Inc., Publishers

World War II and the Post-War Years | President Roosevelt's Fireside Chats

Name: _____ Date: _____

President Roosevelt's Fireside Chats

Read the information below and answer the questions.

During World War II, President Roosevelt gave speeches to the American people over the radio. These speeches were called "fireside chats" because the president liked to think that Americans were sitting in a room with him around a crackling fire.

In his fireside chat on February 23, 1942, President Roosevelt told Americans that everyone on the "home front" would need to pitch in. He asked Americans to build 60,000 planes, 45,000 tanks, and 20,000 antiaircraft guns within the next year. That was equivalent to building an airplane every four minutes, a tank every seven minutes, and two ships a day!

The government needed rubber, which could be melted down and made into life rafts, jeep tires, airplane parts, and gas masks. People collected car tires, garden hoses, rain slickers, and even galoshes.

1. Why didn't the president speak on television? _____

2. What could Americans do to existing factories to start building planes, tanks, and guns? _____

3. What are galoshes? _____

4. People held scrap drives to collect metal. What kinds of metal items do you think people donated to a collection center? _____

5. People were asked to "Use it up, wear it out, make it do, or do without." Why do you think this slogan was so successful? _____

© Mark Twain Media, Inc., Publishers

World War II and the Post-War Years America's Response

Name: _____ Date: _____

America's Response

Americans responded positively to President Roosevelt's request. Read each item below and decide if it is an example of "Use it up," "Wear it out," "Make it do," or "Do without." Place a check mark (✔) in the appropriate box. Some items have more than one answer.

	Use it Up	Wear it Out	Make It Do	Do Without
1. Certain foods like sugar, meat, and butter were needed by soldiers, so those items became scarce at home. The government issued food ration stamps to ensure that food was distributed fairly. Women sorted and traded stamps with each other for what they needed.				
2. Americans did not use the telephone in the evenings, so that men and women in the military could make calls.				
3. Americans altered clothes rather than buy new ones. Hemlines on skirts were let down over and over.				
4. Americans did not waste any vegetables from their gardens. They canned extra vegetables to use in winter.				
5. Americans kept their houses at 65 degrees or lower to save on heating fuels.				
6. Americans stayed on daylight saving time all year. They saved electricity by using fewer lights.				
7. Gasoline for cars was scarce. Some people used horses and wagons.				

Your answers might be different from your classmates' answers. Discuss your ideas together. What is the "spirit" behind the slogan?

© Mark Twain Media, Inc., Publishers

World War II and the Post-War Years

V is for Victory

Name: _____ Date: _____

V is for Victory

Read the information and answer the questions below.

During World War II, the slogan "V is for Victory" became very popular in the United States. Americans often showed the "V" with their index and middle fingers.

The idea was started by a Belgian who had escaped to England after Belgium was occupied by German troops. During radio broadcasts, he encouraged Belgians to write the V sign everywhere they could as a show of defiance against Nazi Germany. He ended each broadcast with the Morse code for "V."

Americans were soon planting *Victory Gardens* and preparing meals from *Victory* cookbooks. There was even a *Victory* game in which players had to draw and trade blocks and chips until they could make the Morse code symbol for "V."

1. Look in a reference book and write the Morse code for the letter "V." _____
   _____

2. Soon, people throughout Europe were writing the letter "V" everywhere. Besides writing the letter, people often sounded out the code. How might they have sounded out the code? Work with a partner to come up with several ideas.
   _____
   _____
   _____

3. What do you think was the effect of so many people in so many countries using "V" as a symbol of victory? Explain your ideas.
   _____
   _____
   _____

4. Girls often wore rhinestone jewelry pins during the war. In what shape do you think these pins were made?
   _____

© Mark Twain Media, Inc., Publishers

World War II and the Post-War Years

Victory Gardens

Name: _____ Date: _____

Victory Gardens

During World War II, the government bought much of the food grown on farms to feed the troops overseas. To provide fresh produce for their families, Americans planted gardens in whatever space they had. Some people just dug up their backyards and planted a garden. Others planted gardens alongside railway tracks and driveways, in parks, on rooftops, and in window boxes. Children planted large gardens in their schoolyards to supply their cafeterias. Factory workers planted gardens as well. These gardens were called **victory gardens** because people believed that by growing their own vegetables, they were helping to win the war. Twenty-one million families had planted gardens by 1942.

In the space below, design a victory garden that includes some of these vegetables: lettuce, carrots, cabbages, radishes, onions, bell peppers, corn, and tomatoes. Draw pictures of the plants in rows. Leave space to walk between the rows. Make a key identifying each plant and the name of the vegetable.

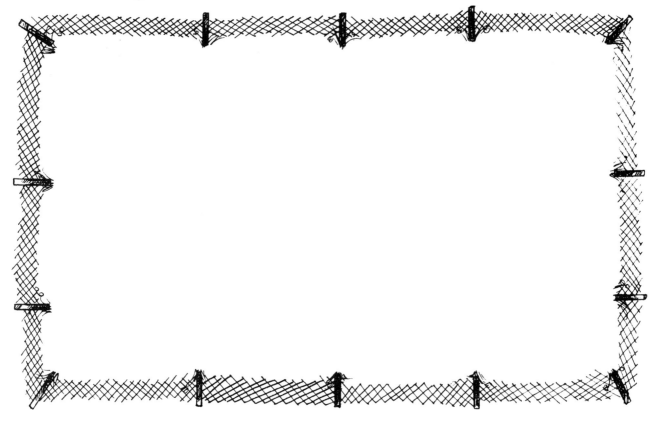

Do one of the following projects:

1. Find out how many days it takes from planting to harvest for the following vegetables: leaf lettuce, carrots, onions, radishes, bell peppers, corn, and tomatoes.

2. Create a recipe for a "victory salad" using some of the vegetables grown in a typical victory garden. You may add dressing, leftover cooked vegetables, and slices of ham, bacon, or chicken.

World War II and the Post-War Years

Wartime Style

Name: _____ Date: _____

Wartime Style

The United States needed to provide millions of uniforms for men and women in the armed forces. Since there wasn't much material left over for those on the home front, Americans made do by creating new kinds of fashions.

Team up with a classmate. Check reference books to find the answers to the questions below.

1. What is a dickey? How was it worn? How did it save material?

   _____

   _____

   Draw a picture of a dickey.

2. Why were hems on girls' skirts let down as many times as possible? What would happen when the hems could no longer be let down? Why were the straps on girls' jumpers made extra long?

   _____

   _____

   _____

3. Girl Scout uniforms used to have long *metal* zippers down the front. Why was the uniform redesigned with buttons?

   _____

   _____

   _____

4. Silk and nylon were needed to make parachutes. Nylon stockings were no longer available. What did women do to make it look as if they were wearing nylons?

   _____

   _____

5. Girls started to wear bobby socks instead of tights because they used much less material. Find out what the word "bob" means.

   _____

   _____

World War II Posters

During World War II, the government printed many posters to persuade Americans to support the war. Some posters tried to motivate people by showing patriotism, confidence, and a positive outlook. This kind of poster used fists, muscles, tools, and artillery to show American strength. Red, white, and blue were often used as the main colors.

Look in books about World War II or on the Internet to find examples of this kind of motivational poster. The slogans on these posters included: "Man the Guns!," "It's a Woman's War, Too!," "United We Win," "Use it Up, Wear it Out, Make it Do, Do Without," and "Four Freedoms."

1. If you were designing a poster, what slogan would you come up with to motivate people to support the war? List two or three slogans on the lines below.

   _____
   _____
   _____

A different kind of poster tried to persuade people to support the war by showing the grim reality of war. This kind of poster pictured gravestones, bloodshed, and corpses. These posters fostered feelings of suspicion, fear, and even hatred toward the enemy.

Look in books about World War II or on the Internet to find examples of this kind of poster. The slogans on these posters included: "Warning! Our Homes Are in Danger Now," "This is Nazi Brutality," "He's Watching You," "He Knew the Meaning of Sacrifice," and "Stamp 'em Out."

2. If you were creating this type of poster, what slogan would you come up with to show people the human cost of war? List two or three slogans on the lines below.

   _____
   _____
   _____

3. Which type of poster do you think was more effective at persuading Americans to support the war? Explain your ideas.

   _____
   _____
   _____
   _____
   _____

World War II and the Post-War Years

Rosie the Riveter

Name: _____ Date: _____

Rosie the Riveter

The poster at the right shows women working in defense plants. **"Rosie the Riveter"** became an expression for any woman working in the defense industry. There was even a song about her: "She's making history working for victory."

1. What did a riveter do?

   _____
   _____
   _____
   _____
   _____
   _____
   _____

2. Why do you think the United States printed posters like this?

   _____
   _____
   _____
   _____
   _____
   _____

3. What effect do you think these posters had on women?

   _____
   _____
   _____
   _____
   _____
   _____

© Mark Twain Media, Inc., Publishers

Name: _____ Date: _____

What Women Did During the War

Before the war, most married women were housewives. Housework alone took about 50 hours each week, and most people felt that it was the woman's job to do it. Read each question below. Check off all the items that answer the question.

1. What happened during the war?

   _____ a. Most women stayed at home.
   _____ b. Women took over many of the jobs that the men had previously done.
   _____ c. Women worked in railroads, steel mills, munitions factories, meatpacking plants, and lumberyards.
   _____ d. Women worked only as typists and waitresses.
   _____ e. Women worked in the defense industries and built B-17 bombers for the war.

2. Why did women go to work during the war?

   _____ a. They needed to support their families because a serviceman's salary was not enough to live on.
   _____ b. They wanted to support the war effort.
   _____ c. They didn't like housework.
   _____ d. Most of the men were gone.
   _____ e. It was just something different to do.

3. What did the War Advertising Council do to instill confidence in women and to encourage them to tackle jobs such as building ships, planes, and tanks?

   _____ a. They put ads in magazines showing dedicated, determined women working in defense plants.
   _____ b. They pictured working women as the heroines of the home front.
   _____ c. They criticized women who didn't work outside the home.

4. Many women worked nine-hour workdays, six days a week. They managed factory work as well as the men had done. What were some of the results of their work?

   _____ a. The women were exhausted because they worked at jobs and at home.
   _____ b. Children learned to take care of themselves.
   _____ c. The women gained independence, confidence, and new skills.
   _____ d. The women greatly aided the war effort.
   _____ e. They hated working.

Women in Uniform

At the beginning of the war, women could only serve in the military as nurses for the army or navy. As more and more men were needed for combat, women were allowed to join the military in noncombat jobs. They worked as parachute packers, postal workers, photographers, clerks, translators, radio operators, weather forecasters, cooks, truck drivers, typists, and mechanics.

The military created new divisions for women including the **WACs**, **WAVEs**, **MRs**, **SPARs**, and the **WASPs**. Match each group with its description on the right.

A. WACs

1. _____ Women's Air Force Service Pilots - These women were highly-trained pilots who flew airplanes in the United States on noncombat jobs. They gave flight lessons, flew cargo and military personnel, and delivered and flight-tested airplanes.

B. SPARs

2. _____ Women's Reserve of the Navy (Women Accepted for Volunteer Emergency Service) - These women served in the United States and Hawaii. They handled the Navy's mail and communications systems.

C. WAVEs

3. _____ S(emper) Par(atus) [Always Ready] - These women served in the U.S. Coast Guard in the United States, Alaska, and Hawaii. They were parachute riggers, radio technicians, storekeepers, bakers, and radar operators.

D. MRs

4. _____ Marine Corps Women's Reserve - These marine reservists worked as radio operators, clerks, mechanics, and chemists in the United States and Hawaii.

E. WASPs

5. _____ Women's Army Corps - These women served overseas and in the United States in hundreds of different jobs.

What Children Did During the War

By 1943, the United States had been fighting the war for two years. It created many changes in the way American children lived. Imagine that you are living in 1943. Answer the questions below in a creative, but realistic way.

1. Who in your family or neighborhood has gone overseas to fight in World War II?

2. How has that made a difference in your life?

3. Is your mother a housewife, or is she working somewhere else now?

4. What type of work does she do?

5. Why is she working?

6. What effect does that have on you?

7. What new responsibilities do you have now?

8. Check off the tasks below that you would do to help the war effort.

    _____ Send letters and presents to patients in war hospitals.
    _____ Trap rattlesnakes to supply venom to protect troops from snakebite.
    _____ Volunteer pet dogs for service.
    _____ Raise carrier pigeons.
    _____ Collect milkweed pods for the fluff to fill life jackets.
    _____ Build model airplanes to teach aircraft recognition to the army and navy.
    _____ Knit mittens, scarves, and socks for soldiers.
    _____ Give up old toys made of rubber or metal so they could be melted down and made into life rafts, jeep tires, airplane parts, and gas masks.
    _____ Participate in scrap drives and collect old pots, pans, foil, and cans.
    _____ Roll bandages.

9. How would you feel if you had helped to support the war effort? Why?

World War II and the Post-War Years   The War Changes the Way Americans Live

Name: _____ Date: _____

The War Changes the Way Americans Live

The statements immediately below list some *effects* of the war on Americans. The statements on the bottom half of the page list what caused those effects. Match the effect to the cause by writing the letter on the correct line.

The Effects

A. Hemlines on skirts became shorter because …

B. New factories were built because …

C. Farmworkers left farms for cities because …

D. More than 27 million people moved during the war because …

E. Thousands of men were drafted because …

F. Women took on jobs because …

G. Children were left to take care of themselves because …

H. People made more money during the war than before the war because …

I. Japanese-Americans were forced to live in internment camps because …

J. Americans planted victory gardens because …

Ration stamps were used for food, gas, and other necessities.

The Causes

_____ 1. they needed to support their families and because the men were in the service.

_____ 2. in the cities, they could get good paying jobs working in factories.

_____ 3. they went to places where there were jobs.

_____ 4. their fathers were in the service, and their mothers were working.

_____ 5. farm produce was needed for the servicemen overseas. People grew vegetables for their families.

_____ 6. there was a shortage of material.

_____ 7. other Americans were prejudiced against them.

_____ 8. they produced so many war supplies.

_____ 9. they were needed to fight in the war.

_____ 10. America needed to build airplanes, weapons, and supplies for the war.

© Mark Twain Media, Inc., Publishers   23

World War II and the Post-War Years

Before and During the War

Name: _____ Date: _____

Before and During the War

In the picture frame on the top, draw a picture of some aspect of American life before World War II. In the picture frame on the bottom, draw a picture of the same aspect of American life during the war. For example, you might draw a picture of what children were doing before the war and what children were doing during the war.

Boot Camp

Name: _____ Date: _____

Read each paragraph below. Identify the problem and the solution in each paragraph.

1. The military could not send untrained men into combat. The men were first sent to boot camp to learn rigorous discipline, combat skills, and team-building skills. Boot camp was also called basic training.

    Problem: _____

    Solution: _____

2. Servicemen often received uniforms that were either too tight or too loose, and nothing was done about it. Their shoes were another matter, however. Everyone needed properly fitted shoes because of the long marches they would undertake. To find the right size for a serviceman's shoes, a supply sergeant would measure a recruit's feet at their widest when he was carrying two buckets of sand. That was roughly equivalent to an infantryman's fifty-pound backpack.

    Problem: _____
    _____

    Solution: _____
    _____

3. Boot camp mixed people together from many different cultural, educational, and religious backgrounds. At first, this resulted in a lot of bullying and prejudice among the men. As they learned to work together and to depend on each other, their prejudice gave way to tolerance, respect, and friendship.

    Problem: _____

    Solution: _____

4. Servicemen needed specialized skills. For example, paratroopers needed to practice jumping from airplanes. Infantrymen needed to learn how to coordinate their assaults with the heavy, mounted guns of the artillery. For this reason, servicemen received more training after boot camp.

    Problem: _____

    Solution: _____

World War II and the Post-War Years

Military Service

Name: _____ Date: _____

Military Service

Use the words in the box to fill in the blanks below. Use reference sources or the Internet to help determine the correct answers.

Army Ground Forces	mechanics	prejudices	GIs	combat
United States	boot camp	World War II	age	Force
volunteered	Americans	400,000		

1. More than 15 million men and women served in the military during _____.

2. About 350,000 women _____ for service as WACs, WAVEs, and as members of other groups.

3. Ten million men went into the _____. Others served in the Marines, Navy, or Coast Guard.

4. About two and a half million men served in the Army Air _____.

5. About a million African-_____ served in World War II.

6. Soldiers were often called _____.

7. During the war, the average _____ of a GI was 26.

8. Seven out of eight GIs were not in _____.

9. The GIs who were not in combat served as _____, drivers, cooks, office workers, instructors, clerks, doctors, and nurses.

10. Four million GIs never left the _____.

11. GIs attended _____ or basic training to learn discipline, combat skills, and team-building skills.

12. Life in boot camp was difficult because the men were homesick, they lacked privacy, they had to learn rigorous discipline, and they were subject to the _____ of the other men who were there.

13. More than _____ Americans died in World War II.

© Mark Twain Media, Inc., Publishers   26

World War II and the Post-War Years   African-Americans in World War II

Name: _____   Date: _____

African-Americans in World War II

Read the information below and answer the questions.

In the 1940s, the United States was still very much a segregated country. African-Americans were not allowed to use the same building entrances, water fountains, and bathrooms as Whites. Black children were not allowed to attend the same schools as White children. Prejudice continued during the war even though more than one million African-Americans were defending America. It was not until 1948 that President Truman banned segregation in the armed forces.

Some African-Americans wondered why they should fight the "White man's war." However, the Nazi racial views and the Japanese treatment of conquered nations made it clear to most minority groups that this was their war too.

In the army, Blacks (the preferred term of the time) served in segregated units. In 1942, ROTC training programs began at Black colleges to train officers, and a flying school for Black aviators was started at Tuskegee, Alabama. By the end of the war, over 80 Black pilots had won the Distinguished Flying Cross, and many Black troops were recognized for bravery and valor during the war. There were also about 4,000 Black women serving with the WACS. Through their dedication and bravery, minority soldiers began to gain the respect of the White soldiers with which they served.

1. Use your own words to write a definition of *segregation*. _____
   _____
   _____

2. How would you feel if you were an African-American soldier during the war who was treated with prejudice?
   _____
   _____
   _____
   _____

3. Why do you think African-Americans fought in the war?
   _____
   _____
   _____
   _____

World War II and the Post-War Years

The Internment of Japanese-Americans

Name: _____ Date: _____

The Internment of Japanese-Americans

Read the passage. Cross out the sentence that does not belong in each paragraph.

1. Even before Pearl Harbor was attacked, many White Americans were prejudiced against Japanese-Americans. After Pearl Harbor, that prejudice increased. The government encouraged this prejudice as a matter of national security. The war in Europe was not going well. Although the Japanese-Americans were loyal U.S. citizens, many people thought they would side with Japan.

2. The basic human rights of Japanese-Americans suffered as a result of this prejudice. Their homes were searched for cameras, radios, and weapons that could be used against the United States. They were assigned numbers and even had to register with the government. In 1942, President Roosevelt ordered the evacuation of Japanese-Americans from the west coast. President Roosevelt lived on the east coast. They had to leave their homes and go to one of ten internment camps in California, Colorado, Utah, Arkansas, and other states.

3. The government wanted everyone to believe that Japanese-Americans were cheerful, and that they accepted the relocation as a wartime necessity. Although Japanese-Americans were not cheerful about leaving their homes, they did cooperate with the government. They were excited to go. They did not protest because they wanted to prove their loyalty to America.

4. The barracks at the internment camps were crowded and provided little privacy. Each family had a small space to live in that was lit by a single light bulb. The families slept on cots. They also had shelves and furniture made from scrap lumber. There weren't any camps in Minnesota. The camps were surrounded by barbed wire and guarded by government troops.

5. After about a year, the Japanese-Americans were allowed to go back home. Unfortunately, many of their old homes and farms had been destroyed. Their property and possessions were gone. Hirohito was still the Emperor of Japan. Many had to start over again looking for jobs and housing. No Japanese-Americans were ever convicted or even accused of spying or treason during World War II. In fact, 33,000 Japanese-Americans served in the American Armed Forces, and two of the most decorated units in the war were made up of Japanese-Americans.

6. In 1980, a government commission reported that the internment of Japanese-Americans was due to "race prejudice, war hysteria, and a failure of political leadership." The commission was made up of fourteen people. The government eventually apologized, and the surviving Japanese-Americans were each given a payment of $20,000.

© Mark Twain Media, Inc., Publishers

Name: _____ Date: _____

Wartime Math

Read each problem and answer the question.

1. During World War II, the government needed money to buy guns, _____
planes, tanks, and ships. Americans were asked to buy war bonds, which were like a loan to the government. A person could buy a war bond for $18.75. Ten years later, the person could redeem the bond for $25.00. How much money did a person earn after ten years?

2. World War II cost the United States $304 billion. One sixth of _____ that cost was paid for by war bonds. How much of the $304 billion was paid for by war bonds?

3. Many women volunteered for the military, including approximately _____ 150,000 WACs; 100,000 WAVEs; 23,000 MRs; 10,000 SPARs; and 2,000 WASPs. In all, approximately how many women served in these divisions of the military?

4. One in eight Americans in uniform experienced combat during _____ World War II. What fraction of Americans in uniform did not experience combat?

5. The Queen Mary could transport as many as 15,000 men each _____ time it sailed from America to Europe. How many trips from America to Europe would the Queen Mary have to make to transport 75,000 men across the Atlantic?

6. Nine hundred forty-one of the 1,162 U-boats commissioned by _____ Hitler were eventually sunk by the Allies. How many U-boats were not sunk?

7. Eleanor Roosevelt was born in 1884. She died at age 78. In _____ what year did she die?

8. Twenty-five thousand women applied to the Women's Air Force _____ Service Pilots (WASPs). Only 1,830 were allowed to serve. How many women were not allowed to serve?

Crossing the Atlantic Ocean

Read the paragraphs below that describe how troops were transported across the Atlantic Ocean to Europe. Then fill in the blanks.

In 1941, airplanes were not yet capable of transporting large numbers of soldiers, tanks, trucks, and food to Europe. That meant that everything had to be transported across the Atlantic Ocean by ship. Several kinds of ships were used, including converted ocean liners and "Liberty Ships."

Ocean liners were former luxury vessels that were refitted with bunks for soldiers. The *Queen Mary,* for example, had been designed to carry about 2,500 luxury passengers. After it was refitted, the ship could carry as many as 15,000 soldiers. The soldiers had to sleep in bunks stacked five high and also had to sleep in shifts. The soldiers received two meals a day, which they often had to eat standing up because of the crowded conditions.

Shipyard employees in the United States worked extra hours to build "Liberty Ships," which could transport both soldiers and thousands of tons of cargo.

Whether the men went across the Atlantic in ocean liners or in Liberty Ships, many suffered from seasickness. Some soldiers were so sick that they could not even stand up. It didn't help that they had a limited amount of drinking water, and that the food was wretched. Both kinds of ships also had to zigzag their way across the ocean to evade German submarines (U-boats). The U-boats laid explosive mines near harbors and torpedoed the ships. The ocean liners did have one advantage, however. They could cross the Atlantic within a week. The Liberty Ships could take as long as a month.

1. What were the two kinds of ships used to transport soldiers across the Atlantic?

2. List three interesting facts about the soldiers' experiences crossing the Atlantic Ocean.

3. Approximate time to cross the Atlantic on a Liberty Ship: _____

4. Approximate time to cross the Atlantic on an ocean liner: _____

World War II and the Post-War Years

The Allies' Strategy

Name: _____ Date: _____

The Allies' Strategy

Read the information below and answer the questions.

Winston Churchill and Franklin Roosevelt

The United States entered World War II after the Japanese attacked Pearl Harbor in December 1941. The United States also had to fight against Germany and Italy because those two nations were joined together with Japan as part of the Axis Powers.

By 1942, Germany controlled Europe from the north to the south. The Germans had also crossed over the Mediterranean Sea to North Africa and had marched northeast from Germany into the Soviet Union. Britain was the only holdout.

Two dozen nations fought against the Axis Powers. Franklin Roosevelt, the President of the United States, and Winston Churchill, the Prime Minister of Britain, were the Allies' representatives. They agreed that their first priority was to defeat Germany and Italy.

Americans took part in the invasion of North Africa in 1942. Led by General Dwight Eisenhower, they took over Morocco and Algeria. They trapped the German troops led by General Erwin Rommel in Tunisia. By May 1943, the Allies had won in North Africa.

The Americans were also part of the Allied invasion of Sicily, an island off the coast of Italy. From there, the Allies invaded the Italian mainland. The Italians were weary of being at war and surrendered to the Allies on September 3, 1943. Mussolini was overthrown, and their king was put back into power. However, German soldiers still occupied most of Italy, so the Allies had to fight their way north to the capital city, Rome. They took control of Rome in June 1944.

1. Why was the defeat of Germany and Italy the top priority for the Allies?

   _____

   _____

   _____

2. What could have happened if Roosevelt and Churchill had decided to give top priority to defeating Japan?

   _____

   _____

   _____

3. Why did the Allies have to continue to fight in Italy after that country surrendered?

   _____

Planning for D-Day

Imagine that you are an American reporter on assignment in England during World War II. In the spring of 1944, you have watched as more than 400,000 American soldiers arrive in England. Everyone expects a big invasion of Nazi-occupied France, but no one knows where or when the invasion will take place. The British and American generals know that this invasion will either make or break the war. The Germans are also expecting the invasion. They build a wall of explosive mines, concrete barriers, and barbed wire along the coast of France.

1. It is now May of 1944. On your own paper, write a short article for your hometown newspaper explaining what has been going on in England and in Nazi-occupied France. Give your readers the facts, but write in a way that lets them anticipate the upcoming invasion.

    The American general, Dwight D. Eisenhower, is in charge of the invasion, which is called Operation Overlord. He has to coordinate men, machines, supplies, ships, planes, weather, tides, and beach conditions. Everything must be perfect, and everything must be kept secret from the Germans. To do this, the Allies set up elaborate deception schemes at Dover to make the Germans think that the invasion will take place at Calais. The Allies park fake inflatable trucks and tanks all around Dover.

2. Use an atlas or reference book to label England, Dover, the English Channel, France, Normandy, and Calais on the map below.

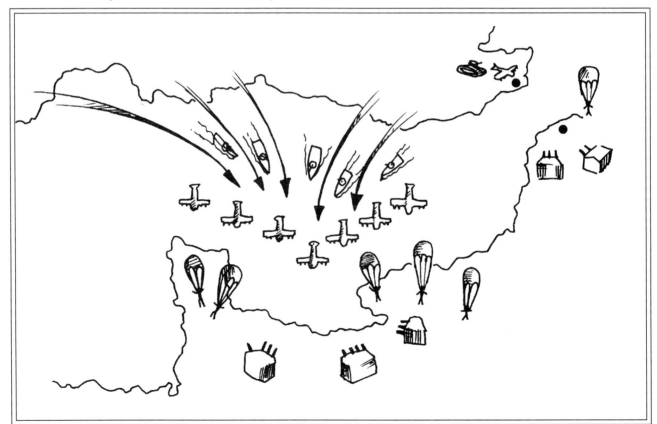

World War II and the Post-War Years

D-Day: The Invasion of Normandy

Name: _____ Date: _____

D-Day: The Invasion of Normandy

Imagine that you are still on assignment in England on June 6, 1944. It is D-Day, and the invasion of Normandy is beginning. The Allies must first cross the English Channel and then begin to drive the Nazis out of France.

The invasion begins before dawn. Hundreds of paratroopers and pilots take off. Almost a million men are on their way. Thousands of ships start across the channel and head for France. In France, French resistance workers help by blowing up bridges, cutting phone lines, and derailing trains full of German soldiers.

As the ships approach the beaches of Normandy, the men climb down ropes onto smaller boats to take them ashore. Each man carries seventy pounds of equipment, and many slip and drown. Most of the first men to reach land are killed by enemy fire.

The Normandy beaches are code-named Omaha, Utah, Sword, Gold, and Juno. On Omaha, the well-trained German troops fire on the Americans from tall cliffs towering over the sand. By the end of the day, the Allies secure all the beaches of Normandy, but at a great price. More than 9,000 men die.

1. Write the headlines for your hometown newspaper for D-Day, June 6, 1944.

   _____

   _____

2. The next day, you ask the war directors at Allied Headquarters in England to tell you whether they consider the invasion a success. What do they say to you?

   _____

   _____

3. You ask a British civilian to comment on the invasion. What does that person say about it?

   _____

   _____

4. Later, you ask a D-Day participant who saw many in his unit die during the invasion to comment. What does he have to say?

   _____

   _____

   _____

© Mark Twain Media, Inc., Publishers

World War II and the Post-War Years

The Infantry in Europe: Part I

Name: _____ Date: _____

The Infantry in Europe: Part I

Read the questions below about how soldiers lived and fought on the European front. Answer each question using a word from the box below. Use reference sources or the Internet to help determine the correct answers.

fog	socks	front	blisterfoot
combat	simple	generals	infantrymen
Army Service Forces			

1. The place where two armies are fighting against each other is called the _____.

2. The United States ground soldiers were called _____. They carried their backpacks and fought on the move.

3. Many infantrymen suffered from "trench foot," which made their feet swell and blister. This condition was a result of wearing wet shoes and leggings for long periods of time. What nickname did the infantrymen gain because of this condition? _____

4. Because the men suffered from trench foot, the army insisted that they receive daily dry _____.

5. The _____ planned their strategy far from the enemy front lines, and then they radioed orders to the commanders at the front.

6. War strategy was _____ on paper. Planes were to bomb enemy positions. Mortar and artillery battalions were to lob shells over the front lines at the enemy, and then the infantrymen were to advance while firing.

7. In reality, war was difficult. Confusion was created by the noise and smoke of the weapons, the shouting of orders by officers, the screams of the wounded, and the shifting positions of the enemy. _____ made it difficult to see, and rainy weather would turn hillsides into slippery slopes.

8. Many men were proud to be soldiers, but no one ever got used to _____.

9. During an assault, troops were supplied with ammunition, water, dry socks, batteries, and food by the _____. They traveled by jeep, foot, or even mule to bring supplies to the front during the night.

© Mark Twain Media, Inc., Publishers

World War II and the Post-War Years

The Infantry in Europe: Part II

Name: _____ Date: _____

The Infantry in Europe: Part II

Read the questions below about how the soldiers lived and fought on the European front. Answer each question using a word from the box below. Use reference sources or the Internet to help determine the correct answers.

| dog food | frostbite | K-rations | toilet paper | portable | GIs |
| rations | backpacks | fire | trucks | | |

1. Soldiers were often called _____, which was short for "government issue."

2. Infantrymen often had to eat cold field _____.

3. Field rations were _____ meals that consisted of a main dish, biscuits, dried fruit, instant coffee, candy, gum, and cigarettes.

4. Individual C-rations came in cans, and _____ were boxed.

5. The C-rations were better than the K-rations, which were often compared to _____ _____.

6. If the infantrymen could build a _____ without attracting enemy shells, they could heat up the canned rations.

7. Sometimes, kitchens on _____ could provide a hot meal.

8. In motorized divisions, soldiers slept in bedrolls in trucks or in tents. Many soldiers, however, slept on a blanket on the ground or in a hole. They used their _____ for pillows.

9. The soldiers were chilled to the bone and sometimes numb with _____ by morning.

10. Even _____ was rationed. Each man received 22 sheets per day.

World War II and the Post-War Years

The Infantry in Europe: Part III

Name: _____ Date: _____

The Infantry in Europe: Part III

Read the questions below about how the soldiers relaxed on the European front. Answer each question using a word from the box below. Use reference sources or the Internet to help determine the correct answers.

| jokes | Red Cross | Stars and Stripes | relax | food |
| baseballs | newspapers | photographs | combat | mail |

1. Combat was exhausting, both physically and mentally. It was important for the men to find ways to _____.

2. Even near the front, soldiers often told _____ as a way to relax.

3. At times, the Army Service Forces brought in _____ so the men could play ball.

4. The _____, an international relief agency based in Switzerland, sometimes traveled to the front to pass out doughnuts or provide entertainment.

5. The army distributed a newspaper called the _____ to the men. It raised their morale because it was written in an upbeat and humorous manner.

6. The army made an effort to deliver the _____ to the soldiers as often as possible.

7. Sometimes, the mail would be several weeks late because the troops were in _____.

8. At times, the men received packages from home with _____ that they shared with their friends.

9. It would lift the men's spirits to receive letters with _____ of their family members and friends.

10. _____ that were sent from their hometowns allowed soldiers to keep up with what was going on at home.

© Mark Twain Media, Inc., Publishers   36

World War II and the Post-War Years — A Letter Home

Name: _____ Date: _____

A Letter Home

The soldiers wrote about their experiences in letters they sent to their family and friends in America. Their letters were censored so that if any letters got into enemy hands, they would not reveal any strategic information.

Imagine that you are a soldier on the front line in Europe. Write a letter to a family member or to a friend in America about your experiences in the war. Use the information you learned in parts one, two, and three of *The Infantry in Europe* or in other reference books. Write about the rations you eat, where you sleep, your combat experiences, and the ways you and the other soldiers try to relax. Use the letter form below.

Research Projects: Part I

Complete one of the following research projects. Then share your report with your classmates.

1. Write a paragraph about the *Queen Mary,* a former luxury ocean liner that was refitted to transport American soldiers across the Atlantic. What was done to the ship so it could transport 15,000 men at a time? What name did Hitler give this ship? How much money did he offer to any German submarine crew who could sink this ship? Was the ship ever sunk?

2. After the soldiers arrived in Europe, they usually did not go into battle immediately. They did, however, go through "culture shock." Write a paragraph about the new customs, languages, and even English expressions with which the soldiers had to become familiar. How were the GIs received by Europeans?

3. Write a letter to a World War II veteran thanking him or her for his or her service to our country.

4. Why were soldiers called GIs? Write a paragraph explaining the origin of this term.

5. GIs wore twin metal "dog tags" around their necks. Write a paragraph explaining what information was contained on the dog tags. Why did the GIs wear them?

6. Interview someone who lived during World War II. Was the person a member of the Armed Services? Which branch? Did the person go overseas or play a supporting role in the United States? What experiences did the person have? If the person was not in the service, what memories does the person have of civilian life on the home front during the war? Write a paragraph summarizing the interview.

7. Find out why the comic strip hero, *Superman,* stayed home from the war. Why did he receive a 4F classification, which meant he was not acceptable for war duty? What did he spend the war doing in the comic strip? Write a paragraph explaining Superman's troubles.

8. How did the Disney Studios influence the war? What were the names of some of the training films Walt Disney made for the army, navy, and other government agencies? What influence did Walt Disney have on the secret D-Day invasion? What was the password for the invasion? Write a paragraph explaining Disney's role in the war.

9. What is V-mail? How did V-mail cut costs? Who used V-mail? Why was V-mail censored before it was sent to the United States? What types of things would be censored in V-mail or in any other kind of mail being sent to the states? Write a paragraph about the importance of V-mail.

World War II and the Post-War Years

The Warplanes

Name: _____ Date: _____

The Warplanes

Read the description of each warplane. Then fill in the blanks using the words in the box.

Japan	avoid	higher	Blitzkrieg	half

1. The **B-17** was the standard, heavy bomber used by the army. It was frequently used in the Philippines. The B-17 could go _____ than any other plane at the time.

2. The **B-29** was the heavy-duty bomber of World War II. It carried eight tons of bombs and could fly at a speed of 360 miles per hour. The

B-29s could saturate an area with bombs. These planes were crucial to the defeat of _____.

3. The English **Spitfires** could actually split enemy planes in _____ because they could fire so many rounds of ammunition per minute. The pilots could go higher than V-1 rockets and explode them in the sky. Most of the Spitfire pilots did not survive the war.

4. Japanese **Zero** fighter planes were extremely efficient planes. Allied pilots tried to _____ these planes.

5. German bombers, called **Stukas**, could drop 1,100-pound bombs with incredible accuracy. They were used in the German _____, which means "lightning war."

© Mark Twain Media, Inc., Publishers

From Ghettoes to Concentration Camps

Read the paragraphs below.

As Hitler's troops invaded other countries, they forced Jewish families to live in isolated parts of town called ghettoes. One-fifth of the people living in ghettoes died of starvation and disease.

Then in 1942, the Nazis built six death camps for the sole purpose of killing Jews and others that Hitler deemed "undesirable." These camps were built in rural Poland because that country had a tradition of anti-Semitism and it was far enough away for secrecy.

There were also concentration camps in Germany where some prisoners worked as slaves for as long as they could live, while others were killed immediately. The sick, the elderly, and the women and children were herded into large rooms where fake showerheads released poisonous gas and killed the people. Afterwards, their bodies were burned in ovens. Nazi scientists also tortured many people in cruel "medical" experiments.

Adolf Hitler not only wanted to clear out all the Jews in Europe, he also wanted to get rid of all those he considered undesirable. He included people who were physically handicapped, mentally retarded, incurably ill, Soviet prisoners of war, Gypsies, criminals, political prisoners, Poles (especially intellectuals), and even Nazis who did not go along with his ways. By the time Germany was forced to surrender in 1945, the Nazis had killed 11 million people, including six million Jews.

Imagine that you are a prisoner at the Auschwitz-Birkenau death camp in Poland. This camp was also a concentration camp and a slave labor camp. On the lines below, write about what has happened to your family since you were brought to the camp. Write about your fears, your expectations, and your hopes. Use your own paper if you need more room.

Did Anyone Help the Jews?

Read each paragraph below. Then choose a title from the box that describes the paragraph. Write the title on the line before the paragraph.

Only Sizable Jewish Community Found in Budapest

German Nazi Saved Jews

Dutch Family Hid 300 Jews on Farm

The People of Denmark Came to the Rescue

1. _____

Oskar Schindler was a German and a member of the Nazi party. He personally saved the lives of 1,300 Jews. He did this by bribing and tricking the Nazis into sparing those who worked in his factories.

2. _____

The Swedish Diplomat Raoul Wallenberg saved thousands of Jews. Because of his work, the city of Budapest, Hungary, was the only city left after the war that still had a large Jewish community.

3. _____

The Bogaard family in Holland hid more than 300 Jews on their farm. Many of them were children.

4. _____

The Danes smuggled almost their entire Jewish population of 7,000 people across the sea to Sweden, which was a neutral nation. There they were safe from the Nazis.

The *Holocaust* is the word used to describe Nazi Germany's killing of six million Jews during World War II.

There were no pictures of the camps until after they were liberated by Americans, and the camps were far away from America, so many people in America didn't believe reports about concentration camps because it didn't seem possible.

Anne Frank

Read the information about Anne Frank and answer the questions.

Anne Frank and her family had lived in Germany, but they fled to Amsterdam, Holland. When Anne was 13, the Nazis began rounding up the Dutch Jews. She and her family hid in the attic of the building where her father had had his spice-importing business. They stayed inside their "Secret Annex" for more than two years. They had to be extremely quiet so they would not be heard by anyone working in the building. Anne spent her time doing homework, learning about her favorite movie stars, and writing in her diary.

1. Imagine that you are a non-Jewish family friend visiting the Secret Annex and that you have a chance to ask Anne Frank three questions. What would you ask her? Write your questions on the lines below.

2. How do you think she would answer your questions? Write her answers on the lines below.

In 1944, when Allied troops were on their way to Amsterdam, someone told the Nazis about the Secret Annex. Everyone there was sent to the concentration camp at Auschwitz-Birkenau in Poland and then on to other camps. Anne's diary was found by a family friend. She saved it for Anne, but Anne never returned. She died of typhus at the Bergen-Belsen concentration camp only two weeks before it was liberated by the British.

Anne had written in her diary, "I feel like a songbird whose wings have been clipped and who is hurling himself against the bars of his cage. I can feel the suffering of millions and yet, if I look up into the heavens, I think that it will all come out right—that this cruelty will end and that peace will return."

3. What must good people everywhere do so that cruelty will end and peace will return?

World War II and the Post-War Years   Joseph Stalin and the Soviet Union

Name: _____   Date: _____

Joseph Stalin and the Soviet Union

Joseph Stalin

Read the information below and fill in the blanks.

    Joseph Stalin was the dictator of the Soviet Union. In 1939, he signed a nonaggression pact with Hitler. They agreed that the Soviet Union and Germany would each take over part of Poland. In addition, the Soviet Union would gain Lithuania, Estonia, and Latvia. Germany and the Soviet Union had been bitter enemies before this time, so with this agreement, Hitler knew he would not have to fight strong enemies on two fronts.

1. What advantage did Germany gain from the pact with the Soviet Union?

   _____
   _____
   _____

2. What advantage did the Soviet Union gain from the pact with Germany?

   _____
   _____
   _____

Read the information below and write a paragraph.

    Hitler broke the pact and invaded the Soviet Union in June 1941. For 18 months, the Germans marched farther into the Soviet Union. The Soviet Union suffered devastating losses, although many of those losses were due to Stalin's poor military decisions and disregard for his soldiers. Stalin did not even train the Soviet troops well. If they were taken prisoner, he called them traitors and did not try to rescue them. Finally, the Soviets were able to stop the German invasion. Later, the Soviet Union became an ally with Britain and the United States in an attempt to defeat Hitler.

    In his own country, however, Stalin was a ruthless dictator. During the time he was in power, 14 million poor peasants died as a result of a famine that he created with artificial food shortages. Another seven to nine million more people were killed by his secret police because they were considered "disloyal." They were either executed or died in Siberian prison camps as a result of slave labor.

    After World War II, Stalin tried to seal off the Soviet Union from the rest of the world. He taught the people to hate anything foreign. He had planned to start World War III at a later time and take over the rest of the world; however, he died of a stroke before he could begin his plan.

Write a paragraph on your own paper using this topic sentence: Joseph Stalin was a ruthless dictator with no regard for human life.

World War II and the Post-War Years

Name: _____   Date: _____

V-E Day

Read each statement below. Put a check mark (✔) next to the correct answer for each statement.

1. After the Allies successfully stormed the beaches of Normandy on June 6, 1944, they began to push the Germans back out of France. The German ground troops were at an advantage because they could
    _____ a. fire from protected positions.
    _____ b. run away.
    _____ c. wear civilian clothes, and no one knew who they were.

2. American infantrymen on the front lines had no choice but to advance in the open, until they were killed, wounded, or
    _____ a. ran away.
    _____ b. retreated back to Normandy.
    _____ c. the war ended.

3. D-Day occurred on June 6, 1944. On August 25, 1944, the Allies liberated Paris. About how long did it take the Allies to reach Paris?
    _____ a. about two weeks
    _____ b. about one month
    _____ c. over two months

4. Six months after D-Day, the Battle of the Bulge took place in northern France. It was one of the bloodiest European battles. The GIs fought bravely, even though they were outnumbered and outgunned. This battle became
    _____ a. Hitler's worst and final defeat.
    _____ b. the Allies' worst defeat.
    _____ c. the Russians' victory.

5. In April 1945, President Roosevelt died. The vice president took over the presidency. The new president was
    _____ a. Douglas MacArthur.
    _____ b. Harry Truman.
    _____ c. Dwight Eisenhower.

6. After the Battle of the Bulge, the Allies marched unopposed toward Germany. The Soviet Union continued their attack on Germany from the east. Hitler knew he was defeated and killed himself in April 1945. Germany surrendered on May 7, and on May 8, the United States declared V-E Day. What does V-E Day stand for?
    _____ a. Victory in Estonia Day
    _____ b. Victory in Europe Day
    _____ c. Victory Everywhere Day

© Mark Twain Media, Inc., Publishers

World War II and the Post-War Years   Crossing the Pacific Ocean

Name: _____ Date: _____

Crossing the Pacific Ocean

Just as some servicemen crossed the Atlantic on their way to fight in Europe, others crossed the Pacific on their way to fight in the Pacific region. The men crossed the ocean on Liberty Ships or on converted ocean liners. Crossing the Pacific on a Liberty Ship could take nearly a month, and some of the men were sick the entire time. The ships had to zigzag across the ocean to avoid Japanese submarines.

Imagine that you are a young man on a Liberty Ship leaving the port of San Francisco. The last sight you see of America is the beautiful Golden Gate Bridge fading into the distance. Write a journal entry for your first day at sea. Describe the scene as well as your thoughts, feelings, fears, and expectations.

World War II and the Post-War Years

The Navajo Code Talkers

Name: _____ Date: _____

The Navajo Code Talkers

In World War II, the military needed to send messages back and forth without the enemy being able to understand the information. To accomplish this task, the military asked Native American Navajos for help.

Four hundred and twenty Navajos served as "Navajo code talkers" during World War II. The code talkers could send messages using the Navajo language. Their language was so complicated that only two dozen non-Navajos in the world understood it. For words that were not in the Navajo language, the code talkers substituted other words. For example, a fighter plane was called a "hummingbird," a submarine was an "iron fish," and bombs were "eggs." The Japanese never found a way to decipher the messages.

1. Devise your own code by writing a symbol or letter under each letter of the alphabet.

   A   B   C   D   E   F   G   H   I   J   K   L   M

   ___ ___ ___ ___ ___ ___ ___ ___ ___ ___ ___ ___ ___

   N   O   P   Q   R   S   T   U   V   W   X   Y   Z

   ___ ___ ___ ___ ___ ___ ___ ___ ___ ___ ___ ___ ___

2. In the space below, write a message to a friend using your code. Try substituting creative expressions for words. For example, you could use the word "disc" for sun. Your friend will need a copy of your code to decipher the message.

© Mark Twain Media, Inc., Publishers

The Japanese Invasion of the Philippines

The day after the Japanese bombed Pearl Harbor, they bombed Clark Field, an American air base in the Philippines. Sixteen thousand American troops and 65,000 Filipino troops, commanded by General Douglas MacArthur, tried to stop the Japanese invasion. Most of the Filipino troops were not trained as soldiers. They were short of food, and their equipment was in bad condition. Thousands of soldiers also died from malaria. The American and Filipino troops were driven back from Luzon to the Bataan Peninsula and the island of Corregidor.

General MacArthur was ordered to leave the Philippines and go to Australia to take over the American offensive against Japan. His famous words were, "I shall return."

On April 8, 1942, 75,000 American and Filipino troops surrendered to the Japanese on the Bataan Peninsula. They were forced to march to prison camps about 85 miles away. Many of the prisoners were already weak from malaria and lack of food. The Japanese soldiers beat the marchers with bamboo poles and clubs. Marchers who fell down due to exhaustion were killed with bayonets. Others were beaten to death. In the next three days, between 3,000 and 10,000 American troops died. This march became known as the Bataan Death March. The Japanese starved the prisoners who survived the march and refused to administer medication to them. The prisoners showed their determination to stay alive by eating whatever they could find, including mice and garbage. The United States was forced to surrender the Philippines to the Japanese on May 8, 1942.

In October of 1944, General MacArthur kept his promise and returned to the Philippines. The Allies had to fight for six months before they regained control of the Philippines.

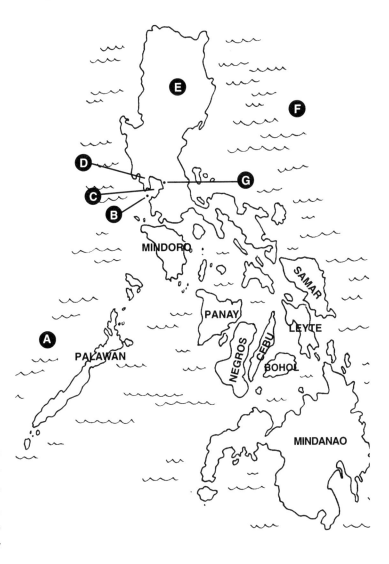

Use a reference book to label the Bataan Peninsula, Corregidor, Luzon, Manila, Manila Bay, South China Sea, and the Pacific Ocean. Write the answers to A–G on your own paper.

Name: _____ Date: _____

Combat in Europe and in the Pacific Region

Read the paragraphs and answer the questions below.

There were significant differences between fighting in Europe and fighting in the Pacific region. In Europe, there were forests, farmlands, and pastures just like in the States. It was easy for the Americans to adjust to this kind of landscape. In the Pacific region, however, the troops had to hack through the dense vegetation of jungles and to watch out for crocodiles and snakes in swamps. Mosquitoes carried malaria and dengue fever.

The American troops and the German troops fought in similar ways. They both used similar military tactics and strategies. Sometimes, the Allies and the Germans allowed a temporary cease-fire so that medics could rescue the wounded. In the Pacific region, the men soon learned that the Japanese fought with no thought of surrender. Their ways of fighting seemed cruel and unfair from an American point of view.

1. What advantage did the landscape in Europe give troops in Europe?

   _____
   _____
   _____
   _____

2. What disadvantage did the landscape give troops in the Pacific region?

   _____
   _____
   _____
   _____

3. Why was it easier to fight against the Germans than against the Japanese?

   _____
   _____
   _____
   _____

Iwo Jima and Ground Zero

Read the information below and answer the questions.

Japan continued to gain control of many Pacific islands. Then in 1942, when the Allies won the Battle of Midway, the tide turned. Between 1942 and 1944, American shipyards built 14 huge, flat-decked aircraft carriers that also served as airplane runways. These carriers helped the Allies to gradually regain control of the Pacific region.

On the tiny island of Iwo Jima, the Marines fought against Japanese troops who believed in "death before dishonor." More than 5,000 Marines died in this battle, and more than 17,000 were wounded. The drawing at the left is from a photo that shows the moment of victory on February 23, 1945. The original photo inspired the creation of a monument to the Marine Corps in Washington, D.C. Inscribed on the marble base of the monument are the words, "Uncommon valor was a common virtue."

After the terrorist attacks on the United States on September 11, 2001, a similar photo was taken of firefighters raising the American flag.

Find a picture of the firefighters raising the American flag at Ground Zero. Then answer the questions below.

1. How are the photos similar? _____

2. How are the photos different? _____

3. What emotions come to mind as you look at both photographs? Write two or three sentences explaining your ideas and feelings about the two photographs.

World War II and the Post-War Years

President Truman's Decision

Name: _____ Date: _____

President Truman's Decision

Read the information below, and then write an opinion paragraph about President Truman's decision to drop the atomic bombs on Japan.

The United States dropped 19 million pamphlets on Japan urging surrender. Food was blockaded from Japan, and many people were dying of starvation; still, Japan would not surrender. Japanese men and women between the ages of 13 and 60 began to mobilize a volunteer army.

It seemed likely that the Allies would next have to invade Japan. General Douglas MacArthur estimated that approximately one million American servicemen would be killed if the Allies invaded Japan. Millions of Japanese would also die in the invasion. With those facts in mind, President Harry Truman made a decision. He authorized dropping two atomic bombs on Japan.

The first bomb was dropped on Hiroshima on August 6, 1945. It killed about 66,000 men, women, and children immediately. Forty thousand more people died later of burns and radiation sickness. The bomb erased an area of about four square miles. Three days later, a second bomb was dropped on the city of Nagasaki. The bombs were devastating, and the effects of the radiation lasted for years.

At the time, most Americans approved the use of the atomic bombs. After people realized how ferocious the bombs were, fewer Americans agreed with their use. Shortly after the bombs were dropped, Emperor Hirohito announced Japan's surrender. August 15, 1945, was declared V-J Day, which stood for Victory over Japan.

The Japanese signing the treaty of surrender on the USS *Missouri*

1. What do you think? Discuss your ideas with your classmates and teacher. Then on the lines below, write a paragraph explaining whether you think President Truman made the right decision. Were there any other alternatives?

_____
_____
_____
_____
_____
_____
_____
_____
_____

World War II and the Post-War Years

The Aftermath of War

Name: _____ Date: _____

The Aftermath of War

Read each statement below. Write "T" for *true* or "F" for *false* in front of each statement. Use the Internet or other reference sources to find the correct answers.

_____ 1. Sixty million people died in World War II.

_____ 2. Forty million of the sixty million people who died were women and children.

_____ 3. Millions of people suffered from mental and physical injuries after the war.

_____ 4. After the war, everyone in Europe and Asia went back to work.

_____ 5. Major cities in Europe were not destroyed.

_____ 6. Beautiful artwork and architecture had been ruined.

_____ 7. People in Japan had almost no food to eat except acorns.

_____ 8. No one in Japan was homeless after the war.

_____ 9. Thousands of people in the Soviet Union lived in hillside dugouts or bombed-out cellars.

_____ 10. More than 400,000 Americans were killed in World War II.

_____ 11. About 700,000 Americans were wounded in World War II.

_____ 12. Many servicemen had psychological problems after the war.

_____ 13. The men who returned home had no trouble readjusting to family life.

_____ 14. Women who had worked during the war all wanted to be housewives again.

_____ 15. Some children had problems readjusting to having a father back in the family.

_____ 16. American soldiers returned to America as heroes.

_____ 17. Two out of every three European Jews died in concentration camps.

_____ 18. The Nazi leaders were not put on trial for war crimes.

_____ 19. Some Nazi leaders were sentenced to death or put in prison.

_____ 20. Some Nazi leaders escaped to South America.

© Mark Twain Media, Inc., Publishers

World War II and the Post-War Years   Life in America After the War

Name: _____   Date: _____

Life in America After the War

Write the cause and the effect on the lines beneath each numbered item below.

1. During the war, people were needed to work in factories to make planes and supplies for the war. Therefore, many people moved from rural areas to cities.

   Cause: _____

   Effect: _____

2. After the war, many women gave up their jobs to men who had returned from the war and needed jobs. Some women hated losing the independence they had gained, but other women were happy to become full-time housewives and mothers again.

   Cause: _____

   Effect #1: _____

   Effect #2: _____

3. People wanted to live near the cities where they worked. Suburbs were built just outside cities to house families.

   Cause: _____

   Effect: _____

4. Planes, tanks, and other war items were no longer needed. Factories now made washing machines, televisions, and refrigerators.

   Cause: _____

   Effect: _____

5. The United States was not invaded during the war, so it was able to continue increasing its manufacturing capabilities. It became the richest and most powerful nation in the world.

   Cause: _____

   Effect: _____

© Mark Twain Media, Inc., Publishers

The United Nations

The United Nations (UN) came into being after World War II in 1945. The UN's main purposes were to preserve peace and security between nations, to solve economic and social problems, and to promote human rights and freedoms.

The UN can investigate a conflict, call for a cease-fire, and set up sanctions (restrictions) against an aggressive nation. It can help calm a crisis and even call on member countries to provide troops for UN forces. These troops can serve as peacekeepers or give military support to a country that has been unjustly attacked.

The UN has had many problems fulfilling its role as a peacekeeper because it often does not have the political, financial, and military support to accomplish its goals.

For example, the UN Security Council usually has not been able to agree on ordering the active force of UN troops. To get an agreement, the five permanent members of the Council—Britain, France, the United States, China, and Russia—must all agree. Any one of these countries can veto a motion. The Council did agree to give military support in 1950 when South Korea was invaded by North Korea. The Council was able to take this action only because the Soviet Union had temporarily left the Council. If the Soviet Union had not left the Council, it would have vetoed the action. The only other time the Council agreed to military authorization was after the Iraqi invasion of Kuwait in 1990.

The UN General Assembly, which consists of delegates from all member nations, also has its problems. The Assembly meets only once a year. Although it can debate any topic, the agreements that it makes are not binding on member states. Some members of the UN also do not pay their membership dues.

Another branch of the UN is the International Court of Justice. International law is unclear and not widely accepted. Not every country accepts the court's authority, and the UN does not have the power to enforce a ruling.

1. Of all the problems listed above, which problem do you think is the most serious for the UN? Why do you think so?

   _____

   _____

   _____

   _____

2. Brainstorm ideas with your classmates about how the UN could become more effective. On your own paper, list at least two of your ideas.

3. In spite of its problems, the UN has helped to keep peace between various countries. Research an example of such a success. Share the information with your classmates.

World War II and the Post-War Years

The Marshall Plan

Name: _____ Date: _____

The Marshall Plan

The countries in Europe were devastated by World War II. They faced famine and economic crisis.

1. What does the word *famine* mean? Define this term using a dictionary.
   _____

2. What does the word *economy* mean? Define this term using a dictionary.
   _____
   _____

3. Why is a strong economy important to a country?
   _____
   _____
   _____

Because the United States was not severely damaged by fighting and its economy was strong, it proposed to help rebuild Europe to ensure a healthy world economy. It was also hoped that a stable economy would lead to political stability in Europe.

4. What does it mean to be *politically stable*? Why was that an important goal after World War II?
   _____
   _____
   _____

George C. Marshall, who was the U.S. Secretary of State in 1947, first called for the United States to assist European countries with their infrastructure. The word *infrastructure* refers to the underlying foundations or framework that makes a system work.

5. Give two examples of *infrastructure* that help make the American economy strong.
   _____
   _____
   _____

Congress passed legislation that was called the Economic Cooperation Act of 1948. It provided monetary aid to help Europe restore its agricultural and industrial productivity. It also helped to increase European trade. This law is commonly known as the Marshall Plan.

The Marshall Plan prevented famine and political chaos in Europe. It also earned George Marshall the Nobel Peace Prize.

© Mark Twain Media, Inc., Publishers

The Korean War

Read the information, and then mark the statements below true or false.

When the Japanese took control of Korea in 1910, they tried to destroy the Korean culture. They would not even allow people to speak Korean or use their Korean names. During World War II, the Allies had promised that Korea would be free after the Japanese were finally defeated.

Japan surrendered to the Allies in 1945. America let troops from the Soviet Union occupy the northern part of Korea because the Soviet leader Joseph Stalin had stated publicly that Korea had the right to be free and have its own government. Stalin's troops marched into the northern part of Korea and then set up a communist-controlled provisional government. The U.S. forces occupied the southern part of the Korean peninsula. The dividing line between the north and south was drawn at the 38th parallel of north latitude.

The United Nations (UN) wanted to supervise free elections in the north, but Soviet guards would not permit UN observers to cross the 38th parallel. Only members of the Communist Party were allowed to vote. Kim Il Sung became the premier of the Democratic People's Republic of Korea in the north. Before the Soviet troops left, they trained the North Korean Army and supplied it with guns, artillery, and heavy tanks.

Free elections were held in the south in 1948, and Syngman Rhee was named president of the Republic of Korea. The U.S. forces left South Korea, with the exception of 500 military advisors. The South Korean Army had little equipment and was not ready for war.

On June 25, 1950, North Korea invaded the south and soon gained control of Seoul. Some historians believe the North invaded because the United States had left Korea, allowing Kim Il Sung an opportunity to reunify the nation.

The United States and 15 other countries joined forces to help South Korea, fighting under the blue and white flag of the United Nations. After three years of furious fighting, it became apparent that neither side would win a total victory on the battlefield. Many discussions were held before a demarcation line, known as the Demilitarized Zone (DMZ), was established between the two sections of Korea at the 38th parallel. A truce between the North Koreans and the UN was signed on July 27, 1953. Guards still remain on both sides of the DMZ, which is two-and-one-half miles wide and extends across the peninsula of Korea.

1. T F The Soviets occupied North Korea in 1910.
2. T F Stalin kept his word and allowed free elections.
3. T F The North Korean Army was well trained and supplied with equipment.
4. T F Korea occupied Japan for many years and tried to destroy its culture.
5. T F Syngman Rhee became the president of the Republic of Korea.
6. T F Free elections means that all citizens of age can vote.
7. T F A communist form of government is still in place in North Korea.
8. T F Korea has recently resolved all of its problems and is reunited.

Research Projects: Part II

Complete one of the following research projects. Then share your report with your classmates.

1. Who developed the coding device called Enigma? What does the word *enigma* mean? How did this device work? When did anti-Nazi forces smuggle an Enigma machine out of Germany? In what year did a team of British cryptographers succeed in cracking the code? What advantage did that give the British? Did the Germans ever find out that the British had the machine and had cracked the code? When did the public learn about Enigma? Write two paragraphs describing Enigma.

2. Which German scientist developed the V-1 missile? What did the "V" stand for? How did the V-1 work? How many V-1 bombs hit London in 1940? How many civilians were killed? Describe the V-1 missile in a well-written paragraph.

3. What role did Eleanor Roosevelt, wife of President Franklin D. Roosevelt, play during the war? What was the name of the newspaper column that she wrote? For what causes did she become a spokesperson? What role did she play in the United Nations? Write two paragraphs about Eleanor Roosevelt, the most famous, admired, and influential woman of her time.

4. What types of things were rationed during World War II? Why was sugar rationed? What could sugar cane be converted into? Why were fuel oil and gasoline rationed? Why weren't women able to wear nylon stockings during the war? What did they do to make it look as if they were wearing nylons? How did the government create a fair rationing plan? Write two paragraphs about rationing during World War II.

5. What part did the American Red Cross play in the war? How did they help soldiers at the front line? What was a "welcome center"? In what countries did Red Cross volunteers work? What did Junior Red Cross members do to aid the war effort at home? Write two paragraphs about the role of the American Red Cross in World War II.

6. Why were dogs recruited for service during World War II? How much did a dog have to weigh? How tall did it have to be? What age did it have to be? How could a dog's sense of smell and hearing help save lives? How did dogs serve on the home front? How did dogs serve overseas in battle? Write two paragraphs about war dogs in World War II.

7. Why did people in America want to see movies during World War II? What types of movies were popular during the war? When was the first movie about Lassie made? How much did it cost to go to the movies? What were the black-and-white newsreels about? How did people in the theater react to the newsreels? Write a paragraph describing the importance of movies during World War II.

World War II and the Post-War Years

Famous Quotations

Name: _____ Date: _____

Famous Quotations

Team up with a classmate. Use reference books to find out who said each quotation. Match the quotation to the person who said it, and write the names on the lines below.

1. "We shall fight on the beaches, we shall fight on the landing grounds, we shall fight in the fields and in the streets, we shall fight in the hills; we shall never surrender."

   _____

2. "What counts is not necessarily the size of the dog in the fight—it's the size of the fight in the dog."

   _____

Dwight Eisenhower

3. "No one can make you feel inferior without your consent."

   _____

4. "A general is just as good or just as bad as the troops under his command make him."

   _____

Winston Churchill

5. "Yesterday, December 7, 1941, a date that will live in infamy—the United States of America was suddenly and deliberately attacked ..."

   _____

6. "The buck stops here."

   _____

General Douglas MacArthur

Eleanor Roosevelt   **Franklin Roosevelt**   **Harry S Truman**

Choose one of the following leaders from World War II: Franklin Roosevelt, Eleanor Roosevelt, Harry Truman, Dwight Eisenhower, General George Patton, General Douglas MacArthur, or Winston Churchill. Gather information from reference books, and write a short biography of that person. Share the biography with your classmates.

© Mark Twain Media, Inc., Publishers

Books About World War II

Many excellent books have been written about World War II. Some examples are Theodore Taylor's *Air-Raid Pearl Harbor,* Lois Lowry's *Number the Stars,* Anne Isaac's *Torn Thread,* and Eleanor Coerr's *Sadako and the Thousand Paper Cranes.*

Choose a book about World War II. Ask your teacher if the book is appropriate before you begin. Read the book, and fill out the form below.

Title and author of the book: _____

_____

Was the book fiction or nonfiction? _____

Where and when did the events in the book take place? _____

_____

Briefly describe the main character. _____

_____

_____

_____

What was the major problem the main character had to face? _____

_____

_____

_____

How was that problem resolved? If it wasn't resolved, why not? _____

_____

_____

_____

_____

Would you recommend the book to your friends? Why or why not? _____

_____

_____

Suggested Reading

Gourley, Catherine. *Welcome to Molly's World—1944: Growing Up in World War II America.* Middleton, WI: Pleasant Company, 1999.

Isaacs, Sally Senzall. *America in the Time of Franklin Delano Roosevelt.* Des Plaines, IL: Heineman Library, 1999.

Jones, Catherine. *Navajo Code Talkers.* Greensboro, NC: Tudor Publishers, 1997.

King, David C. *World War II Days.* New York, NY: John Wiley & Sons, Inc., 2000.

Krull, Kathleen. *V is for Victory.* New York, NY: Alfred A. Knopf, 1995.

Kuhn, Betsy. *Angels of Mercy.* New York, NY: Athenum Books for Young Readers, 1999.

Nicholson, Dorinda Makanaonalani. *Pearl Harbor Child.* Kansas City, MO: Woodson House Publishing, 1993.

Skipper, G.C. *MacArthur and the Philippines.* Chicago, IL: Children's Press, 1982.

Stanley, Jerry. *A True Story of Japanese Internment: I am an American.* New York, NY: Crown Publishers, Inc., 1994.

Welch, Catherine A. *Children of the Relocation Camps.* Minneapolis, MN: Carolrhoda Books, Inc., 2000.

Whitman, Sylvia. *Uncle Sam Wants You!* Minneapolis, MN: Lerner Publishing Company, 1993.

Zeinert, Karen. *The Incredible Women of World War II.* Brookfield, CT: The Millbrook Press, 1994.

Answer Keys

The Rise of the Dictators (p. 3)
1. A dictator is someone who is in complete control of a country and often rules it unjustly.
2. ruthless, authoritative, selfish, greedy, power-hungry, egotistic, etc.
3. Some people may not want to think for themselves or take responsibility for problems. They may hope the dictator will solve problems for them.

The German Dictator (p. 4)
A. France
B. Belgium
C. Great Britain
D. the Netherlands
E. Denmark
F. Germany
G. Poland
H. Czechoslovakia
I. Austria

The Italian Dictator (p. 5)
1. 1922
2. National Fascist Party
3. empire
4. Ethiopia
5. Albania
6. Hitler
7. Japan

Map:
A. Mediterranean Sea
B. Italy
C. Albania

The Japanese Dictator (p. 6)
A. China
B. Manchuria
C. Japan
D. Hawaiian Islands
E. Pacific Ocean
F. Philippine Islands

Which Dictator? (p. 7)
1. H 2. T 3. M 4. M 5. H 6. T 7. M
8. H 9. T 10. M 11. T 12. M 13. H 14. T
15. H

The War Begins (p. 8)
1. Germany, Italy, Japan
2. Europe
3. Greater East Asia
4. Britain, France
5. 1939
6. Two dozen (24)
7. The United States
8. Allies

The Persecution of the Jews in Germany (p. 9)
1. mongrel: an animal, especially a dog, that is a mixture of different breeds
2. scapegoat: someone who is unfairly made to take all the blame for something
3. anti-Semitic: prejudiced against Jews
4. synagogue: a building used by Jewish people for worship and religious study
5. emigrate: to leave your own country in order to live in another one

Britain Stands up to Hitler (p. 10)
1. Hitler would have taken complete control of Europe.
2. Answers will vary.
3. Lights would give bombers a target.

Should the United States Join the Allies? (p. 11)
Answers will vary.
Reasons to join: If Germany defeated Britain, the United States would have to fight anyway. The Axis Powers could gain control of the oceans and limit shipping between the Allies and other nations.
Reasons not to join: Many Americans were still recovering from the Depression. They were out of work and needed to take care of their own problems. The United States had recently fought in World War I and was not ready to fight again. Isolationists were opposed to helping foreign countries. America felt protected by the Atlantic and Pacific Oceans.

The Attack on Pearl Harbor (p. 12)
1. The United States joined the Allies immediately.
2. They were not able to defend the naval base.
3. It was easy for the Japanese to succeed because there was no resistance.
4. The planes were destroyed. The pilots could not get airborne.
5. Since there was no one to stop them, the Japanese simply took over island after island in the Pacific.
6. America had to fight in Italy and Germany, too.

President Roosevelt's Fireside Chats (p. 13)
1. Television was not yet available.
2. Existing factories would have to be converted so they could manufacture planes, tanks, and guns. New factories would also have to be quickly built.
3. waterproof shoes that fit over ordinary shoes to protect them from rain or snow
4. pots, pans, tinfoil, cans, old toys, etc.
5. It was a catchy slogan. It made people feel they could help bring about victory overseas.

V is for Victory (p. 15)
1. . . . — (dot, dot, dot, dash)
2. Whistling, knocking on doors, honking car horns, tapping pencils, etc.
3. People became united in their goal to obtain victory.
4. V shape

World War II and the Post-War Years — Answer Keys

Wartime Style (p. 17)
1. A dickey was a removable collar. It was worn instead of a blouse under a sweater to save material.
2. The hems were let down over and over so the skirt could still be worn even as a girl grew taller. After no more hem could be let down, the girl just wore a shorter skirt. The straps were extra long so they could be adjusted as a girl grew taller.
3. Metal was needed for the war effort.
4. Women used leg makeup.
5. The word "bob" means to shorten.

Rosie the Riveter (p. 19)
1. Riveters worked in teams. One woman shot a rivet (a strong metal bolt) into a metal plate with a gun, and another woman flattened it on the opposite side.
2. Women were needed to work in factories. The poster tried to give women confidence.
3. The posters inspired, motivated, and encouraged women.

What Women Did During the War (p. 20)
1. b, c, e   2. a, b, d
3. a, b   4. a, b, c, d

Women in Uniform (p. 21)
1. E   2. C   3. B   4. D   5. A

The War Changes the Way Americans Live (p. 23)
1. F   2. C   3. D   4. G   5. J   6. A
7. I   8. H   9. E   10. B

Boot Camp (p. 25)
1. **Problem:** Untrained men could not be sent into combat.
   Solution: The men were sent to boot camp.
2. **Problem:** Everyone needed properly fitted shoes.
   Solution: A supply sergeant would measure a recruit's feet at their widest when he was carrying two buckets of sand.
3. **Problem:** Men bullied each other because of their different backgrounds.
   Solution: Prejudice ended when they learned to work together and depend on each other.
4. **Problem:** Servicemen needed specialized skills.
   Solution: They received more training after boot camp.

Military Service (p. 26)
1. World War II   2. volunteered
3. Army Ground Forces   4. Force
5. Americans   6. GIs
7. age   8. combat
9. mechanics   10. United States
11. boot camp   12. prejudices
13. 400,000

The Internment of Japanese-Americans (p. 28)
1. The war in Europe was not going well.
2. President Roosevelt lived on the east coast.
3. They were excited to go.
4. There weren't any camps in Minnesota.
5. Hirohito was still the Emperor of Japan.
6. The commission was made up of fourteen people.

Wartime Math (p. 29)
1. $6.25   2. $50.67 billion
3. 285,000   4. 7/8
5. 5   6. 221
7. 1962   8. 23,170

Crossing the Atlantic Ocean (p. 30)
1. Refitted ocean liners and Liberty Ships
2. Answers will vary.
3. Month
4. Week

The Allies' Strategy (p. 31)
1. Hitler had to be stopped.
2. Hitler could have gained control over Britain.
3. Italy was occupied by German troops.

Planning for D-Day (p. 32)
2.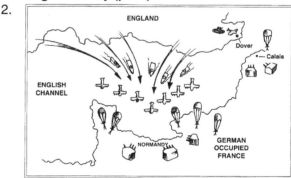

The Infantry in Europe: Part I (p. 34)
1. front   2. infantrymen
3. blisterfoot   4. socks
5. generals   6. simple
7. Fog   8. combat
9. Army Service Forces

The Infantry in Europe: Part II (p. 35)
1. GIs   2. rations   3. portable
4. K-rations   5. dog food   6. fire
7. trucks   8. backpacks   9. frostbite
10. toilet paper

The Infantry in Europe: Part III (p. 36)
1. relax
2. jokes
3. baseballs
4. Red Cross
5. Stars and Stripes
6. mail
7. combat
8. food
9. photographs
10. Newspapers

The Warplanes (p. 39)
1. higher
2. Japan
3. half
4. avoid
5. Blitzkrieg

Did Anyone Help the Jews? (p. 41)
1. German Nazi Saved Jews
2. Only Sizable Jewish Community Found in Budapest
3. Dutch Family Hid 300 Jews on Farm
4. The People of Denmark Came to the Rescue

Joseph Stalin and the Soviet Union (p. 43)
1. The Germans didn't have to fight against the Soviets and the Allies at the same time.
2. The Soviets took part of Poland. They also obtained Lithuania, Estonia, and Latvia.

V-E Day (p. 44)
1. a 2. c 3. c 4. a 5. b 6. b

The Japanese Invasion of the Philippines (p. 47)
A. South China Sea   B. Corregidor
C. Manila Bay   D. Bataan Peninsula
E. Luzon   F. Pacific Ocean
G. Manila

Combat in Europe and in the Pacific Region (p. 48)
1. The landscape in Europe was similar to the land in America. Americans knew what to expect.
2. The landscape in the Pacific region was unfamiliar to most Americans. They had no experience hacking through thick vegetation in jungles or fighting crocodiles in swamps.
3. The Germans had similar military tactics and strategies. Japanese fighting seemed cruel and unfair.

The Aftermath of War (p. 51)
1. T 2. T 3. T 4. F 5. F 6. T 7. T
8. F 9. T 10. T 11. T 12. T 13. F 14. F
15. T 16. T 17. T 18. F 19. T 20. T

Life in America After the War (p. 52)
1. **Cause:** People were needed to work in factories.
   Effect: People moved to cities.
2. **Cause:** Women gave up their jobs to men.
   Effect #1: Some women hated losing independence.
   Effect #2: Some women enjoyed being full-time housewives again.
3. **Cause:** People wanted to live near their work.
   Effect: Suburbs were built.
4. **Cause:** War items were no longer needed.
   Effect: Appliances were now manufactured.
5. **Cause:** The United States increased its manufacturing during World War II.
   Effect: It became the richest and most powerful nation in the world.

The Marshall Plan (p. 54)
1. Famine: a serious lack of food
2. Economy: the way a country runs its industry, trade, and finance
3. When a country has a strong economy, people are employed and make enough money for necessities.
4. A country that is politically stable has a government that protects the rights of all of its citizens. This kind of country would not be in danger of takeover by a dictator. The countries in Europe were not politically stable after World War I, and that allowed Hitler to control Germany and then take over many other countries.
5. Any two: steel industry, electric power, telephones/communication, roads, water systems, etc.

The Korean War (p. 55)
1. F 2. F
3. T 4. F
5. T 6. T
7. T 8. F

Famous Quotations (p. 57)
1. Winston Churchill   2. Dwight Eisenhower
3. Eleanor Roosevelt   4. General MacArthur
5. Franklin Roosevelt   6. Harry S Truman